MILET
WORDWISE

CHEESE PLEASE, CHIMPANZEES

Fun with Spelling

Tracy Traynor

Illustrated by Lily Bronfeyn

Milet Publishing, LLC
333 North Michigan Avenue
Suite 530
Chicago, IL 60601
info@milet.com
www.milet.com

Cheese Please, Chimpanzees: Fun with Spelling
Text by Tracy Traynor
Illustrations by Lily Bronfeyn

First published by Milet Publishing, LLC in 2008

ISBN 978 1 84059 511 6

Printed and bound in China

Please see our website **www.milet.com**
for other Milet Wordwise titles.

MILET
WORDWISE

CHEESE PLEASE, CHIMPANZEES

Fun with Spelling

Tracy Traynor

Illustrated by Lily Bronfeyn

The seahorses n**eighed**,
the spider crabs pl**ayed**
and the merm**aid**
drank lemon**ade**.

A dog with
green **eyes**
won second pr**ize**
for his
clever disgu**ise**.

Let me introd**uce**
my g**oose**.
He loves
chocolate m**ousse**
and pineapple j**uice**.

My friend J**oel**
has a m**ole**.
He sleeps
in a fishb**owl**
and likes
rock and r**oll**.

The photogr**aph**
of h**alf**
a gir**affe**
made me
laugh!

I
saw a sp**y**
with a funny bow-t**ie**
flying up h**igh**.

Here's
a great souven**ir** —
a toy reind**eer**
with a p**ier**ced
ear.

A sn**ow**man
called J**oe**
g**oe**s
to hot Mexic**o**.
He should kn**ow**
that's a *really*
bad idea...**Oh**, n**o**!

I th**ought**
I had c**aught**
a fish —
but guess what?
It was really
a polka-dot astron**aut**!

You,
cockat**oo**,
d**o** you come from Per**u**?
You are purple and bl**ue**,
with only one sh**oe**.

Pl**ease**,
chimpanz**ees**,
don't squ**eeze**
my ch**eese**!

MAGIC SPELL

Spelling can be fun. There are lots of different ways you can spell some sounds.

Here are a few of them...

Words that sound like...

reind**eer**
sp**ear**
sph**ere**
p**ier**
souven**ir**

merm**aid**
w**eighed**
marmal**ade**
spr**ayed**
ob**eyed**

g**oose**
Br**uce**
m**ousse**
j**uice**

disgu**ise**
dragonfl**ies**
b**uys**
s**ighs**
pr**ize**
eyes
d**yes**

astron**aut**
b**ought**
t**aught**

spy
hi
goodbye
sigh
eye
guy
pie

chimpanzees
tease
sneeze
Japanese
Louise
monkeys
cheese
skis
seize
peas
he's

snow
toe
although
owe
yo-yo
sew
whoa

cockatoo
gnu
glue
threw
you
too
through
canoe
to
two

mole
bowl
goal
hole
stroll
Joel
patrol

giraffe
calf
laugh
autograph